P9-CSU-643

My 10 Day Green Smoothie Cleanse Protein Recipes: 51 Clean Meal Recipes to help you After the 10 Day Smoothie cleanse!

by **Jessy Smith**

Copyright © 2014 by: Jessy Smith

All rights reserved. This book or any portion thereof may not be reproduced or used in any manner whatsoever without the express written permission of the publisher except for the use of brief quotations in a book review.

Disclaimer:

The information provided in this book is designed to provide helpful information on the subjects discussed. The publisher and author are not responsible for any specific health or allergy needs that may require medical supervision and are not liable for any damages or negative consequences from any treatment, action, application or preparation, to any person reading or following the information in this book.

Table of Contents

INTRODUCTION
Let's Get Started
Yummy Broccoli Vinaigrette
Fresh Wrapped Fish
Steak-Fried Chicken
Apple Stew and Autumn Chicken
Scrumptious Shrimp Meal
Baked Fish and Vegetables
Baked Salmon and Vegetables
Grilled Chicken Wraps
Grilled Lemon Salmon
Southwestern Scallop
Asparagus Chicken Salad
Delicious Sea Scallops
Yummy Kale with chicken broth
World Greatest Egg Salad
Mushroom Omelet
Scrambled Egg and Vegetable Wrap-ups
Over-D-Top Oven Shrimp
Shrimp and Cucumber Stir-Fry
Shrimp n Mushroom Stir-Fry
Spinach n Chicken Salad
Orange Glazed Chicken Wings
Festive Scrambled Eggs
Avocado Kale Salad
Avocado Salmon Salad
Caribbean-Spiced Roast Chicken
Curried Chicken Salad
Fontana Chicken Pesto Pizza
Black Bean Pizza
Ultimate Fried Eggs
Lime Broiled Catfish
Pumpkin and Shrimp
Brown's Simple but Delicious Fish
Crunchy Vegetables with Chicken
Balsamic Pepper Chicken
Mushroom Chicken
Chicken Parmesan

Almond Chicken Salad
Smoky Salmon Spread
Macadamia Nut Chicken
Sesame Green Beans
Tasty Chicken Egg Foo Young
Delicious Fried Eggs with Red Wine Vinegar
Baked Spiced Chicken
Shrimp Stir-Fry
Southern Mushroom Soup
Thai Chicken Salad
Fish with Mediterranean Salsa
Slow Cooker Chicken Curry with Quinoa
Quinoa Pudding with Vanilla
Quinoa with Almond Porridge
Thank You
Other Health Related Book You'll Like

INTRODUCTION

The 10-DAY green SMOOTHIE CLEANSE is a phenomenal program developed by a leading weight loss expert. People in the program are seeing result, losing as much as 15+ Pounds in 10 Days. So don't be left out in this life changing program that would help you lose weight, look younger, detoxify your body, boost your immune system and burn your belly fat.

After the 10 days of cleanse and detox, you'll be noticing some changes in your weight, it is imperative that you stay on track and don't lose it. To effectively stay on track you should eat a high protein food so as to keep your weight on check and achieve great result thereafter.

We have prepared delicious and healthy meals that are clean and high in protein and in line with the 10 day green smoothie Cleanse, which would help you with weight loss after the 10 days smoothie cleanse.

Let's Get Started

Sometime, it's hard to keep to a routine of Dieting when you are always lost on Food to eat to keep you in line. These Over 50 Clean and high-Protein Recipes we have prepared would help with your weight loss and aid you stay healthy after the 10 day green Smoothie Cleanse.

However, if you don't like an ingredient in any of the meal, **You are free to tweak or substitute this recipes based on your personal preference,** you can substitute it with other similar ingredients, as long as it's under the clean meals prescribed in the 10 day green smoothie cleanse. You can also make your own variation.

We have tried our best to bring you the best clean meals Recipe for the 10 day green smoothie clean plan, but sometimes, it's impossible to get it all right, So if you come across any error whatsoever in this book, please don't hesitate to send me a mail at jessysmith@cleanproteinRecipes.com. Your thoughts and feedback is important to me and it's very much welcome.

Now on to the Recipes:

Yummy Broccoli Vinaigrette

Servings: 6

What you need:

1/2 teaspoon dry mustard

2 tablespoons white vinegar

1 teaspoon olive oil

1/4 teaspoon sea salt

1/4 teaspoon ground black pepper

1 1/2 pounds fresh broccoli

How You Make It:

1.   Wash broccoli; lower stems and trim leaves.

2.   Cut broccoli into spears. Steam until crisp-tender, for about 5 minutes. Drain.

3.   Combine vinegar, pepper, oil, mustard, and sea salt.

4. Drizzle over broccoli. Serve immediately.

5. Also good chilled as cold leftovers.

Fresh Wrapped Fish

Servings: 4

What you need:

3 tablespoons capers, drained

4 large stalks celery, thinly sliced

3 tablespoons fresh lemon juice

1/2 teaspoon ground black pepper

1/2 teaspoon sea salt

2 tablespoons fresh parsley

4 rectangular pieces of parchment paper

2 tablespoons dill

2 pounds fresh white fish fillets

How You Make It:

1. Distribute sliced celery evenly in the center of each parchment paper lay out.

2. In small bowl, mix lemon juice, capers, sea salt, parsley, pepper, and dill together.

3. Sprinkle each with a teaspoon or so of caper mix.

4. Divide fish fillets among the 4 papers.

5. Divide remaining caper mix evenly over each fillet.

6. Gather paper together in center. Fold tightly.

7. Twist ends securely to seal.

8. Bake in 400° oven for 20 minutes.

9. Packets will be slightly browned and puffed.

10. Slide packets onto dinner plates.

11. Open each Serving when you want to use.

Steak-Fried Chicken

Servings: 8

What you need:

1 pound sliced fresh mushrooms

2 teaspoons olive oil

1 bunch scallions, chopped

1/2 teaspoon sea salt

8 boneless, skinless chicken breast

1/2 teaspoon ground black pepper

1/2 cup chicken broth

2 tablespoons chopped fresh parsley

How You Make It:

1. In large skillet, heat olive oil.

2. Sauté mushrooms and scallions for about 2 minutes.

3. Remove from pan. Set aside.

4. Pound chicken breasts to one-quarter-inch thickness.

5. Sprinkle with sea salt and pepper.

6. Sauté in same pan, about four minutes on each side.

7. Spread mushroom mixture over chicken breasts. Pour broth over chicken.

8. Cover, bring to a boil, and then quickly reduce heat.

9. Simmer until chicken is tender, for about 3-4 minutes.

Apple Stew and Autumn Chicken

Serves 4

What you need:

3 carrots, peeled, sliced

1 chicken, cut in parts

1/4 cup apple cider vinegar

1/2 tsp. nutmeg

6 apples, peeled, sliced

6 whole cloves

1 cup shredded cabbage

1/2 tsp. sea salt

1/4 tsp. pepper

2 tsp. Dijon mustard

1 cup applesauce

1 3/4 cups low sodium chicken broth, warm

How You Make It:

1. Heat large Dutch oven over medium high temperature, after spraying with vegetable cooking spray.

2. Add chicken turning to brown on all sides, and cook, about 10 minutes.

3. Sprinkle with nutmeg, pepper and sea salt.

4. Spread mustard over chicken pieces; add warm broth, cloves, carrots and vinegar; bring to a boil.

5. Reduce heat to low, Cover and cook 15 minutes.

6. Add apples and cook for about five minutes.

7. Add cabbage, stirring into liquid. Cook, covered, until fork can be inserted in chicken with ease, about 10 minutes more.

8. With slotted spoon, remove vegetables and chicken to warm serving bowl and keep warm.

9. Stir applesauce, into liquid; boil on high temperature for about 5 minutes and pour over chicken and vegetables.

10. Serve with brown rice, if desired.

Scrumptious Shrimp Meal

Servings: 8

What you need:

3 tablespoons fresh lemon juice

1 clove garlic, grated

1/4 teaspoon cayenne pepper flakes

¼ teaspoon ground white pepper

1 medium head cabbage, grated

2 pounds medium shrimp, peeled

1/4 cup fresh lime juice

2 tablespoons chopped fresh basil leaves

1/2 teaspoon sea salt

How You Make It:

1. In medium bowl, stir together cayenne pepper, garlic and lemon juice.

2. Sprinkle white pepper over the top. In lemon mixture, marinate the shrimp for about 20 minutes.

3. Meanwhile, mix together the sea salt and lime juice and toss with the cabbage.

4. Cook the shrimp pan with the marinade until pink for 2 to 3 minutes.

5. Make a shallow well in the center and toss cabbage briefly.

6. Mound the shrimp in the middle of the cabbage.

7. Garnish with additional cayenne pepper flakes and basil, if desired.

Baked Fish and Vegetables

Servings: 8

What you need:

2 cloves garlic, grated

1 head cauliflower

1 red pepper

2 green peppers

1 teaspoon crushed dried rosemary leaves

1 pound whole mushrooms

2 pound salmon fillets

2 teaspoons olive oil

1 tablespoon white vinegar

1/4 teaspoon ground black pepper

1/2 teaspoon sea salt

How You Make It:

1. Steam cauliflower for about a minute, after separating into florets. Drain thoroughly.

2. Cut the peppers into one-inch squares, after seeding.

3. Clean mushrooms; trim ends.

4. Combine cauliflower, mushrooms, peppers, rosemary and garlic, in a large baking dish.

5. Toss with olive oil.

6. Bake until vegetables are crisp-tender at 400° for 15-20 minutes.

7. Cut salmon into one-inch chunks.

8. Add to vegetable mixture.

9. Return to oven and bake until fish flakes easily with fork, for an additional 10-12 minutes.

10. Sprinkle fish mixture with pepper vinegar, and sea salt. Toss lightly.

Baked Salmon and Vegetables

Servings: 8

What You Need:

1 pound whole mushrooms

1 head cauliflower

2 cloves garlic, grated

2 green peppers

2 teaspoons olive oil

1 red pepper

1/2 teaspoon sea salt

1 teaspoon crushed dried rosemary leaves

1/4 teaspoon ground black pepper

2 pound salmon fillets

1 tablespoon white vinegar.

How You Make It:

1. Separate the cauliflower into florets. Steam for a minute.

2. Drain thoroughly.

3. Seed peppers, cut into one-inch squares.

4. Clean mushrooms; trim ends.

5. In a large baking dish, combine peppers, mushrooms, cauliflower, rosemary and garlic.

6. Toss with olive oil. Bake at 400° for 15-20 minutes, until vegetables are crisp-tender.

7. Cut salmon into one-inch chunks.

8. Add to vegetable mixture. Return to oven and bake an additional 10-12 minutes, until fish flakes easily with fork.

9. Sprinkle fish mixture with vinegar, sea salt, and pepper. Toss lightly.

Grilled Chicken Wraps

Servings: 4

What You Need:

Vegetable cooking spray

2 teaspoons oregano

2 tablespoons fresh lemon juice

4 thin slices peeled onion

1 green pepper, seeded and quartered

4 large lettuce leaves

1/4 cup chopped fresh mint

4 boneless, skinless chicken breast halves, rinsed, patted dry, and pounded thin

How You Make It:

1. Brush chicken breasts on both sides with lemon juice, after you've heated the grill.

2. Sprinkle with oregano.

3. Remove grill top and lightly coat with cooking spray. Return to grill.

4. Arrange chicken breasts and onion slices on grill. Cook, turning once, 5 to 6 minutes per side, until chicken juices run clear when prodded with a tip of a sharp knife.

5. Onion slices and pepper quarters should take about 2 to 3 minutes per side.

6. Transfer onions and peppers to a carving board and cut into strips.

7. When chicken is done; transfer to carving board and cut into 1/2-inch strips. Keep warm.

8. Divide the chicken, pepper, and onion strips on the center of each lettuce leaf, sprinkle with mint, and roll up.

9. Secure with toothpicks if necessary.

Grilled Lemon Salmon

Servings: 8

What You Need:

3 tablespoons lemon juice

8 salmon steaks (about 3 pounds)

1 tablespoon olive oil

3 cloves garlic, grated

1 teaspoon sea salt

1/2 teaspoon ground black pepper

How You Make It:

1. Mix all ingredients except salmon in a shallow glass baking dish.

2. Arrange salmon in baking dish, turning once so both sides are covered with the marinade.

3. Refrigerate for about 30 minutes. Heat grill.

4. Grill salmon until fish flakes easily with a fork, about 5 minutes per side.

5. Serve hot.

Servings: 5 main dish

What You Need:

1/4 teaspoon ground black pepper

1 tablespoon dill

5 Belgian endive leaves

2/3 cup water

1/4 cup shredded Swiss cheese

2 tablespoons mayonnaise

1/2 pound bay scallops

2 tablespoons cream cheese

1 teaspoon prepared mustard

1 egg white, room temperature

How You Make It:

1.   Dry and set aside endive leaves after washing.

2. Boil scallops until no longer translucent, in 2/3 cup water.

3. Takes about 5 minutes. Drain thoroughly and cool.

4. Cream together mayonnaise, cream cheese and Swiss cheese.

5. Stir in dill, ground black pepper and mustard. Fold in well-drained scallops.

6. Beat egg white at high speed until stiff peaks form, using an electric mixer.

7. Do not over beat.

8. Fold egg white gently into scallop mixture. Spoon scallop mixture among endive leaves.

9. Arrange in baking dish. Bake at 425° until puffy and golden for 8 to 10 minutes. Serve immediately.

10. Cut each endive leaf into 4 wedges for appetizers.

Asparagus Chicken Salad

Servings: 8

What You Need:

1/2 pound boneless, skinless chicken breast

1/2 pound steak

2 pounds asparagus

4 hard boiled Omega-3 eggs, quartered lengthwise

1/2 pound mushrooms, sliced

1 teaspoon olive oil

4 oz. Swiss cheese

2 tablespoons finely chopped onion

1 head romaine lettuce.

How You Make It:

1. Poach chicken breast in small amount of water until thoroughly cooked. Drain. Cool thoroughly.

2. Cut into ½-inch strips. Set aside. Grill steak to desired doneness. Cool thoroughly.

3. Cut into ½-inch strips. Set aside. Break woody ends off asparagus. Rinse.

4. Cut into bite-sized pieces and place in a microwave-proof casserole dish.

5. Cover with plastic wrap, and microwave for 2 minutes.

6. Carefully remove plastic wrap. Plunge asparagus in cold water. Drain completely. Sauté mushrooms in 1 teaspoon olive oil for 1 minute. Remove from pan. Set aside to cool.

7. In medium glass or plastic bowl, toss cheese, chicken, steak, and onion.

8. Add asparagus and mushrooms when thoroughly cool.

9. Pour 3 tablespoons dressing over asparagus mixture. Chill for 1 hour.

10. Meanwhile, tear lettuce leaves into salad bowl. Rinse, and cover with ice water.

11. Chill while asparagus mixture is chilling.

12. Drain lettuce thoroughly. Arrange lettuce in salad bowl.

13. Pour reserved asparagus mixture over lettuce.

14. Arrange egg quarters over salad. Stir remaining dressing.

15. Serve salad with dressing.

Note: Leftover meats may be substituted for fresh cooked chicken and steak.

Delicious Sea Scallops

Servings: 8

What You Need:

3 pounds Sea Scallops

2 tablespoons almond butter

1 1/2 pound fresh spinach

3/4 cup grated Gruyere

2 tablespoons finely chopped scallions

3/4 cup heavy cream

½ teaspoon sea salt

¼ teaspoon ground black pepper

3 large Portobello Mushrooms

How You Make It:

1. Sauté scallions until tender.

2. Heat One teaspoon almond butter in saucepan. Add cream.

3. When sauce begins to thicken, stirring constantly, add cheese.

4. Add pepper and sea salt to taste, keep warm.

5. Wash spinach thoroughly. Sauté spinach in half the remaining almond butter.

6. Arrange on serving plates. Clean and stem mushroom.

7. Slice mushrooms, and sauté in same pan for 1 to 2 minutes.

8. Arrange mushrooms over spinach.

9. Add remaining almond butter to pan. Sauté scallops 1 1/2 to 2 minutes on each side in same pan.

10. Arrange scallops on mushrooms. Spray reserved sauce over scallops. Serve immediately.

Yummy Kale with chicken broth

Servings: 4

What You Need:

2 tablespoons chicken broth

1 pound kale

11/4 teaspoon sesame oil

¼ teaspoon ground black pepper

2 garlic cloves, grated

How You Make It:

1. Remove tough stems, after washing kale in several changes of water.

2. Cut into one-inch squares.

3. Heat the sesame oil, in a wok or frying pan.

4. Stir-fry the garlic but do not allow it to brown.

5. Add the chicken broth and kale.

6. Cover until kale wilts, for about 2-3 minutes.

7. Sprinkle with ground black pepper.

World Greatest Egg Salad

Servings: 4

What You Need:

1/4 cup finely chopped dill pickle

8 hard boiled Omega- 3 eggs, chopped

1 teaspoon chopped fresh parsley

1/4 cup finely chopped celery

1 scallion, finely chopped1/3 cup mayonnaise

Dash pepper

1/4 teaspoon sea salt

4 large lettuce leaves

How You Make It:

1.   Mix all the ingredients leaving only the lettuce leaves and parsley.

2.   Chill. Just prior to serving, Pile on lettuce leaves.

3.   Sprinkle with parsley.

Mushroom Omelet

Servings: 1

What You Need:

2 eggs

2 cups sliced fresh mushrooms

1 teaspoon olive oil

2 tablespoons grated cheddar cheese

1 tablespoon chopped scallions

How You Make It:

1. Sauté mushrooms until almost ready to give up their liquid, in a little olive oil.

2. Remove from pan and set aside. Beat eggs.

3. Pour into same pan and cook over medium heat until partly solid.

4. Sprinkle with cheese, scallions and half of the mushrooms.

5. Fold over and continue cooking until hot. Top with rest of mushrooms. Serve.

Scrambled Egg and Vegetable Wrap-ups

Servings: 8

What You Need:

1 teaspoon olive oil

2 scallions, chopped

1 tablespoon onion, chopped

1 green pepper, chopped

2 cups sliced mushrooms

8 romaine lettuce leaves

1/2 teaspoon ground black pepper

1 tablespoon taco seasoning mix, dry

4 eggs and 4 egg whites, or 8 eggs

3/4 cup shredded cheddar cheese.

How You Make It:

1. Coat a large skillet with olive oil. Sauté green pepper, onion, and mushrooms until tender.

2. Transfer vegetables to small bowl. Stir in scallions. Set aside.

3. On serving plates, sprinkle lettuce evenly with cheese.

4. Beat together eggs and egg whites. Stirring often, until just firm and moist, in same skillet cook eggs.

5. Divide eggs among lettuce leaves.

6. Divide vegetable mixture over eggs.

7. If necessary, roll up the lettuce leaves and secure them with toothpicks. Serve immediately.

Over-D-Top Oven Shrimp

Servings: 8

What You Need:

1/4 teaspoon freshly ground black pepper

2 pounds large fresh shrimp, raw, deveined

2 teaspoons almond butter

2 teaspoons olive oil

2 cloves garlic, minced

1 tablespoon chopped fresh parsley

How You Make It:

1. In a large bowl, combine garlic, almond butter, oil, and pepper.

2. Add shrimp and toss lightly to coat.

3. Spread shrimp, in a single layer, in a shallow, oven-safe casserole dish.

4. Broil shrimp for about 3-4 minutes, approximately 4-inches from the heat.

5. Turn shrimp, and broil for an additional 3-4 minutes (or until lightly browned).

6. Sprinkle with chopped fresh parsley and serve.

Shrimp and Cucumber Stir-Fry

Servings: 4

What You Need:

2 large cucumbers, peeled

3 tablespoons sunflower oil

2 tablespoons minced fresh ginger

1 clove garlic, minced

1/4 cup minced scallions

1 pound medium shrimp, shelled and deveined

Sea salt to taste

1 tablespoon white vinegar

How You Make It:

1. Cut cucumbers in half lengthwise; scrape out and discard seeds.

2. Cut each cucumber half crosswise into 1/4 inch thick slices.

3. Heat wok over high heat.

4. When wok is hot, add 1 tablespoon oil. When oil is hot, add cucumbers and 1 tablespoon of the ginger; stir-fry 2-3 minutes until cucumbers are tender-crisp.

5. Arrange on serving platter. Keep warm.

6. Pour remaining oil into wok.

7. When oil is hot, add garlic, remaining 1 tablespoon ginger, scallions, and shrimp.

8. Stir-fry about 3 minutes, until shrimp is pink and cooked through.

9. Sprinkle with sea salt and pour vinegar over shrimp. Stir briefly, and arrange over cucumbers.

Shrimp n Mushroom Stir-Fry

Servings: 4

What You Need:

2 cups sliced mushrooms

1 teaspoon sesame oil

1 teaspoon olive oil

1 clove garlic, grated

1/2 teaspoon grated fresh ginger

1 cup okra

1/2 cup chopped green peppers

2 cups string beans

1/4 teaspoon ground black pepper

2 cups cleaned cooked shrimp

How You Make It:

1. Combine and Heat Stir-fry mushrooms, garlic, peppers, and ginger in sesame oil and olive oil until crisp-tender.

2. Meanwhile string beans and steam okra until crisp-tender.

3. Drain, and add to peppers and mushrooms.

4. Stir in shrimp and pepper until just warmed.

5. Serve over a bed of lettuce.

Spinach n Chicken Salad

Servings: 8

What You Need:

1/2 pound fresh sliced mushrooms

1/2 pound fresh spinach

4 cups cooked, diced chicken

2 tablespoons olive oil

3 tablespoons white vinegar

1/2 teaspoon poppy seeds

1/4 teaspoon dry mustard

How You Make It:

1. In small bowl, combine vinegar, mustard, oil, and poppy seeds together.
2. Refrigerate.
3. Wash spinach and tear into bite size pieces.
4. Add mushrooms and chicken. Serve.

Orange Glazed Chicken Wings

Serves 2

1 tbsp. vegetable oil

18 chicken wings, tips removed and wings cut in half at joint

1/2 cup orange marmalade

1/4 cup Dijon mustard

2 tbsp. soy sauce

How you make it:

1. Heat the oil in a large skillet over medium-high heat.

2. Add the wing pieces, and fry until golden brown on all sides, about 6 t
   o 10 minutes.

3. Spoon off any excess fat, and add the orange marmalade, mustard
   and soy sauce to the skillet, stirring to blend the ingredients and coat the
   wing pieces.

4. Simmer on medium heat 8 to 10 minutes, until
   the sauce thickens and glazes the wings.

5. Serve hot.

Festive Scrambled Eggs

Serves 4

What you need:

12 eggs

1 1/2 cups milk, divided

1/2 teaspoon sea salt

1/4 teaspoon pepper

2 tbsp. diced pimientos

2 tbsp. minced fresh parsley or chives

2 tbsp. all-purpose flour

1/4 cup almond butter or margarine

How you make it

1. In a large bowl, beat eggs and 1 cup milk.

2. Add the sea salt, pepper, pimientos and parsley.

3. In a small bowl, combine flour and remaining

    milk until smooth; stir into egg mixture.

4. In a large skillet, melt almond butter over medium heat.

5. Add egg mixture.

6. Cook and stir over medium heat until the eggs are completely set.

Avocado Kale Salad

Yield: 2 servings

What you need:

½ cucumber, sliced

1 handful **almonds**

½ head of **kale**

1 **avocado**

1 handful radishes, sliced

Sea sea salt, to taste

½ lemon, squeezed for juice

How you make it:

1. Sauté (toss) the kale and avocado, using your hands.

2. Then add the radishes, cucumbers, and almonds.

3. Finally toss the salad with lemon juice and sea sea salt.

Avocado Salmon Salad

What you need:

1 ounce feta cheese, crumbled

2 (6 ounce) fillets salmon

1/4 cup Almond butter, melted and divided sea salt and pepper to taste

4 ounces fresh mushrooms, sliced

12 grape tomatoes, halved

2 tbsp. olive oil, divided

5 sprigs fresh cilantro, chopped

8 ounces leaf lettuce, torn into bite-size pieces

1 avocado - peeled, pitted, and cubed

1 fresh jalapeno pepper, chopped

2 tbsp. distilled white vinegar

How you make it:

1. Preheat the oven broiler.

2. Line a baking sheet with aluminum foil.

3. Place the salmon on the foil, and brush with 2 tbsp. melted almond butter.

4. Season with sea salt and pepper.

5. Broil 15 minutes, until fish is easily flaked with a fork.

6. Melt the remaining almond butter in a skillet over medium heat, and sauté the mushrooms until tender.

7. Place the tomatoes in a bowl, and drizzle with 1 tbsp. olive oil.

8. Season with sea salt and pepper.

9. Toss together the mushrooms, avocado, salmon, tomatoes, lettuce, cilantro, and jalapeno, in a large bowl.

10. Pour small amount of the remaining olive oil and the vinegar over the surface.

11. Add sea salt and pepper Seasoning to taste, and spread with feta cheese to serve.

Serves 4

What you need:

1 1/2 tbsp. fresh lime juice

2 fluid ounces rum

1 tbsp. brown sugar

1/4 teaspoon cayenne pepper

1/4 teaspoon ground clove

1/2 teaspoon ground cinnamon

1/2 teaspoon ground ginger

1 teaspoon black pepper

1/2 teaspoon sea salt

1/2 teaspoon dried thyme leaves

1 (3 pound) whole chicken

1 tbsp. vegetable oil

How you make it:

1.   Preheat oven to 325 º F (165 º C).

2. In a small bowl, combine the lime juice, rum, and brown sugar; set aside.

3. Mix together the cayenne pepper, clove, cinnamon, ginger, pepper, sea salt, and thyme leaves.

4. Brush the chicken with oil, then coat with the spice mixture.

5. Place in a roasting pan, and bake about 90 minutes, until the juices run clear or until a meat thermometer inserted in thickest part of the thigh reaches 180 ° F.

6. Baste the chicken with the sauce every 20 minutes while it's cooking. Allow chicken to rest for 10 minutes before carving.

Curried Chicken Salad

What you need:

3 cups diced cooked chicken breast meat

6 slices bacon

1/2 cup chopped celery

1 cup seedless grapes

1 cup mayonnaise

2 tbsp. red onion, minced

1/2 tsp. curry powder

1 tsp lemon juice

1/2 tsp. Worcestershire sauce

Sea salt and pepper to taste.

How you make it:

1. In a large, deep skillet, place bacon. Cook until evenly brown over medium high heat.

2. Crumble and set aside.

3. Combine bacon, chicken, celery, and grapes, in a large bowl.

after graduation, or maybe to Europe. It was a helluva long time ago, you know."

"Were you close friends?"

"Well, we hung out together a pretty fair amount, I guess, but I wouldn't say we were best buddies."

"You must've made an impression on him, because he asked for you specifically."

Jim sat back, shaking his head. Graham returned from the rest room and sat down next to Allenson.

"What do you want me to do?" Jim asked.

Allenson closed the file and put it back in her bag. "The director wants me to bring you to Langley, where you'll be thoroughly briefed and prepared."

"Prepared for what?"

Allenson lifted her eyebrows. "We'll be heading overseas."

"You mean…where did you say this guy is now, Somalia?"

"That's where he is, and so that's where we'll be going."

Graham gave her a look, as close to showing emotion as Jim had seen from him. Jim figured this was the first time the FBI agent had heard this part of the story.

"You're leaving something out," Jim said.

"What's that?"

"The part where you say, 'Should you or any of your Impossible Missions Force be caught or killed, the secretary will disavow any knowledge of your actions.'"

Allenson leaned forward. "Look, Mr. Hayes, this is no joke. This is a critical matter of national security—"

Jim stared right back at her. "Hey, I've got a job here. I've got a big project due pretty soon and my boss is on my ass about it. You want me to tell her I'm taking a few days off to go chasing terrorists?"

"You can't tell anyone about this operation," she said.

"You'll recall that when we sat down here, you agreed our conversation would be confidential."

Jim looked away again, trying to sort it out. On the one hand, it sounded like the most bizarre thing he'd ever heard. Joe Shalita, a terrorist? The guy wouldn't have hurt a fly back then. But that was a long time ago, and people changed, sometimes drastically.

He looked back at the agents, trying to decide if they were legit. He supposed it could be part of some elaborate prank, but who would go to the trouble to hire two people to pull off a charade like this? One way to make sure was to have them take him to the FBI headquarters in Chicago. Did the CIA actually have an office anywhere outside Virginia?

If this crazy story was true, if Joe had turned himself into this Sudika character and now he wanted to defect, then he must have some very important intelligence to hand over, otherwise the government wouldn't be playing ball with him like this. They'd just lure him into a trap and snatch him, send him off to one of those secret prisons he was always hearing about, and that would be that. Why would they need to come all the way to Wisconsin to enlist the help of Jim Hayes?

"So you're telling me this is an officially sanctioned mission?"

The CIA agent nodded. "Mr. Hayes, less than twenty-four hours ago I was sitting in the Oval Office, watching the President of the United States review your file."

"I didn't know I had one," Jim said.

"Everybody's got a file," the FBI agent said. That bought him a sharp look from Allenson.

She turned back to Jim. "This operation has been personally authorized by the president," she said. "Now, I need an answer from you."

"I have to use the rest room," he said, standing up. He really did, but he also needed some space. He felt his heart rate accelerating, and forced himself to calm down and breathe regularly.

In the men's room, Jim took care of his immediate business, then looked in the mirror as he washed his hands. He tried to imagine what Allenson and Graham were seeing when they looked into the eyes he was seeing now. Did they see a guy who was skeptical, puzzled, maybe a bit frightened? That's what Jim saw.

He had to give these people an answer. Part of him was saying he should tell them to get lost, forget it, go solve their own problems. He had a life here in Cedar Lake, a home. He had a job, although lately he'd been wondering if it was one he wanted anymore. He had Gina, or at least a shot at something with her. There was his daughter in Milwaukee, and maybe this guy she was dating would give her a ring, and he'd have grandchildren. That was certainly something to live for, wasn't it?

If he went along with these people, he might never hold his grandchild. What if he went over there and things went to hell and he had to act? Could he do it? Practicing in the dojo or at Systema camp was one thing, coming face to face with a terrorist who wanted to kill you was quite another. Even worse than that terrible morning in the church. Not a spot for an amateur to be in. This was a job for professionals.

Like his brother.

The door opened and a man came in, snapping Jim out of his thoughts. He quickly left the rest room and walked down the short hallway back into the coffee shop. The agents were still in the booth, talking together, no doubt telling themselves that this guy didn't have what it takes.

The flat-screen TV on the wall was showing something that caught his eye. It was the silhouette of a man, standing against a cloudy sky, holding a sword straight out. It was an ad for the Marines, one he'd first seen a few nights before.

Marines in dress blues with M-1 rifles, the Silent Drill Team, stood near a lighthouse, then in Times Square. Jim strained to hear the audio.

"There are those who dedicate themselves to a sense of honor...to a life of courage..." Most in the coffee shop ignored the TV, but at one table, a gray-haired man was staring up at the screen, and a tear was rolling down his cheek. Next to him, his wife patted him on the hand. Had he been a Marine? Where had he been? Maybe Chosin Reservoir, or Khe Sanh.

Mark had been in a lot of places. Bosnia, Iraq, Afghanistan, probably more, doing dangerous things, noble things. Where had Jim been, what had he done? He'd always wondered what he would do when the chips were down.

Like they were now.

He made his way back to the booth. The agents looked at him, and he could see their skepticism. He looked away and gathered himself, then back at them. "You probably know my brother's in the Army," he said quietly.

"Yes," Allenson said. Graham remained silent.

"I tried to get in the Reserves," Jim said. "They wouldn't take me. Bad knee. The Marines wouldn't, either. My country said sorry, you're not good enough. But now it seems the country has changed its mind." He paused, thinking of his father, his brother.

"Okay," he said, looking directly at the CIA agent. "When do we leave?"

CHAPTER TWENTY-ONE

AFGHANISTAN

I T WASN'T IN Mark's nature to take a day off, but today he had to force himself to take it easy. Off-days weren't that common downrange anyway, although he made sure his troops got in as much R&R in as possible. Out here it wasn't like it had been back in Vietnam, when guys could get a couple days' leave and head to Saigon or maybe Bangkok. From what he'd been told, those were wild times. If you were out here, the only city to speak of was Kabul, and that wasn't exactly regarded as a playground. But the medical people were finding out a lot about PTSD and said getting rest and some measure of recreation while deployed was vital. Mark wasn't about to disagree.

It took a lot of self-discipline. Alcohol wasn't allowed, porn stashes were discouraged, although Mark knew better than to think those rules were universally obeyed. He told his company commanders to cut the men a little slack. Every now and then somebody pushed the envelope a little far, and there were consequences. Sometimes serious ones, especially if the offense involved civilians. Fortunately, Mark hadn't had to deal with anything like that during his time as C.O. of Roosevelt. So far.

It was nearly twenty-four hours after the firefight at the farmhouse and his headache seemed to be a little quieter. There was an angry bruise on his left temple, but the doc said there didn't appear to be any internal damage. He cautioned Mark to be aware of any concussion symptoms, and made sure Ruiz and the rest of the staff were keeping an eye on him. All in all, Mark could live with the headache. If the bullet had been another inch or so to the right it would've made sure that he'd never have headaches again.

Things appeared quiet in the valley, so Mark set out to make his usual Sunday-morning rounds of the base first thing after breakfast. It was warming up already, maybe to about seventy-five today. Hot, but not Iraq-in-the-summer hot. He'd had enough of that, and up here in the mountains there was usually enough wind to keep it from getting stifling. The air was clear, too, unlike the odor of Iraq—combustion fumes, garbage, Lord knew what else. You got used to the heat, you expected it to be hot all the time, but the stench hit you in the face as soon as you stepped off the plane and it took a while to get used to that. It was much better here, although some villages had their own special aromas, and Kabul's pollution was legendary.

Dealing with the weather was easy, but the culture shock was something else entirely. Mark had been all over the country and sometimes it seemed like he was on another planet, maybe a cross between the moon and Mars, except it was warmer and you could breathe the air, sort of. For that matter, the people were like aliens in many respects. The way they talked, dressed, ate, how sometimes the men wiped their ass with a bare hand, how they treated their women. Mark had wondered many times, during his first tour, just what the hell they were doing here, why they bothered with these people. Clean out the bad guys and move on, that's what should've been done.

Gradually, though, his perceptions changed. Yes, they were a different people, but people were different all over, just more so here, and a lot of it had to do with geography. Landlocked, scarce in resources, the Afghans for centuries had been forced to scratch a living out of hardscrabble conditions that made cotton sharecroppers back in the American Deep South look like aristocrats. When you got right down to it, as tough as his life was, the average Afghan wanted what the average American wanted, the average Brit, Russian, Chinese, whatever. He wanted to make a living and raise his family and live in peace.

Over here, sometimes, it appeared that was too much to ask. Since Alexander's day, foreign armies had moved through these valleys and plains, seeking out not plunder but strategic advantage. Whoever held Afghanistan in those days could dominate the trade routes of southern Asia. These days, it wasn't much different. If America could leave this place in friendly hands, that would not only cut al-Qaida off from its once-secure sanctuaries, but it would give America and the West strategic access to this part of the world for decades to come. Mark looked to the north. Up there, the Caspian Sea basin was one of the world's biggest reserves of oil and gas. The Russians had once controlled that, but not now. It was up for grabs. Mark wondered sometimes if that was the real reason he and his fellow soldiers were here.

Whatever the reason, it was tough, demanding duty. One of the biggest challenges for Mark and his fellow officers was keeping their men, and themselves, focused and healthy. Perhaps more than any other conflict in American history, this war was taking a psychological toll on the men and women who fought it, and their families back home. The isolation over here was a serious problem, but in a curious way, Mark believed it was also a strength. With few distractions, maintaining focus was easier than it might've been in earlier wars. The camaraderie among the men here was stronger than anything Mark had experienced before. From the day you arrived here you looked forward to going home, and you knew that the only way to survive lay with your comrades. If you had your buddy's back, he had yours, and you just might make it home alive. And downrange, you needed to trust your buddies because you sure as hell couldn't trust anyone else you would encounter, not even the men of this land you helped train and mentor.

That was the real tragedy, Mark knew now, after spending so much time here. It baffled the Americans, sometimes enraging them to the point where they did things they would not normally think of doing. No matter how much you interacted with the people here, they never fully accepted you. Not like the Germans and Japanese had done. How many Americans came home from those conquered nations with native-born brides? More than a few, but Mark had not heard of a single American marrying an Afghan woman.

They were here because this job, as hard as it was, as distasteful as it felt, had to be done. The enemy who had come to his country to slaughter his people had come from places like this, using them as sanctuaries for training, breeding grounds for hate. Mark was proud of the work his country had done in Afghanistan, and in Iraq too, toppling brutal dictatorships and giving millions a fighting chance to live in peace, but he wondered where it would all end, if it would ever end.

Mark's headache wasn't being improved by this kind of thinking, so he shoved it aside and moved on, out into the main area of the base. Focus on the little things, he reminded himself. There were people way above his pay grade to take care of the big things.

Camp Roosevelt covered about fifty acres on a plateau near the north end of the valley, offering a commanding view. The Russians had realized its strategic importance when they built the first base here back around 1980. Many of their buildings were standing when the Americans arrived, and the engineers had whipped things into pretty decent shape in the years since. It was still on the primitive side compared to Army posts in Europe or back in the States, or even the big one in Kandahar, but it would do.

There were troops out jogging around the perimeter, and Mark supposed that somebody would rustle up enough guys for touch football later in the day. There would probably be some action around the spider pit; sometimes men on patrol would capture camel spiders, non-poisonous arachnids as big as a man's hand, bring them back to the base and match them up in combat with heavy bets riding on the outcomes. Several men waved at him as they ran by, and a few asked how he was doing. Word had gotten around quickly about the firefight.

He came to one of the lookout posts on the perimeter. Nearby, a group of soldiers was working on the wire fencing. Getting the fence squared away in the beginning had been a bitch, but it had to be done. It was in sad shape when he got here, but Mark knew the history of this base in the Soviet days. They'd been lax about the wire and paid for it one night when the *muj* attacked, rocketing the poorly-secured guard posts and breaching the perimeter. Learning from that lesson, he'd ordered the fencing reinforced and HESCO barriers erected at the four corner guard posts. Mark was glad to see that the four men on duty here this morning weren't sleeping or otherwise screwing around. "Good morning," he said.

One of the privates, a new man, stood up and was raising his hand in salute when the corporal pulled him back down. "Goddamn it, Carson, get down," he said. "You don't salute out here at the wire! You want to show every friggin' raghead sniper on that mountain that we got an officer here?" He turned casually toward Mark. "Good morning, sir," he said, nodding.

"As you were," Mark said, kneeling down in the sand-bagged dugout. "How's it going, Mandli?"

The corporal, who'd been here a few months longer than Mark, took off his helmet and wiped a sleeve across his high forehead. The kid couldn't be more than twenty-five but he was already losing his hair. "Pretty quiet, sir. Some movement out there, but nothing out of the ordinary."

"That's good. Maybe it'll be a quiet day. We could use one of those, couldn't we?"

"Could use more than one, you ask me, sir."

"Can't argue with that. Let's see what we got." The dugout was shielded by HESCOs, wire mesh containers lined with fabric, then filled with dirt. Some of the smaller FOBs had HESCOs around the entire perimeter, but here Mark had just installed them at the four corners, in the center of the north side, and flanking the entrance gate on the south. Mark hauled himself up onto the ledge of the dugout, looking out over the valley. The view was breathtaking. On the mountainside directly ahead, about two miles away, he could see a small herd of goats, with three upright figures guiding them along. Mark took the binoculars offered by Mandli and zeroed in on them. Looked like one adult man and two boys, picking their way effortlessly along a trail that was probably older than all of them put together.

Mark chatted with his men for a few minutes, then stood up and stretched, enjoying the growing warmth of the sun. An inner voice told him to stay low, beware of snipers, but he figured he'd had his close call for the week yesterday. "Say, Colonel," Mandli said, "could I have a word with you, sir?"

"Sure." They walked a few paces away. "What's on your mind, soldier?"

"Well, sir, we got a new guy in our company, Asian kid, Korean, I think he is…" Mandli stopped, then looked away for a second, biting his lower lip.

Mark had a feeling he knew what was coming. Mandli had a rep for being a stand-up guy, definitely sergeant material. "Speak your mind, Corporal. This is just between us."

The slender young man sighed. "Well, sir, there's some guys in the company, they've been giving Hong a lotta shi—I mean, they've been giving him a hard time."

"Why? Because he's Asian?"

Mandli nodded. "Yes, sir. He's the only Asian in the company. Aren't too many on the whole base, I don't think. Anyway, there's only a few characters doing this, and the lieutenant's been on their ass about it, but last night, well, it kinda got worse, some name-calling, things like that. Nobody deserves that kind of treatment, you ask me. I'm afraid one of these times, somebody's gonna get popped and it'll be real trouble. Besides, Hong's a nice guy, pretty quiet, keeps to himself. Can't say that about everybody in the company, sir, to be honest with you."

"All right. What's your company?"

"Company C, sir. I hope I'm not speaking out of turn, sir. The lieutenant's a good guy. I don't want to say he's not doing his job."

Mark checked his watch. Divine services were starting in

about fifteen minutes at the base chapel, and he knew Winkler would be there. "Don't worry about it. I'll have a word with the lieutenant, and I'll keep your name out of it."

"Thank you, sir."

Around 1500, Mark was finishing up an e-mail to Eddie, wondering how long it would take his son to respond this time. Sometimes it was the next day, usually longer. He owed one to Jim, too. It had been a little awkward last night, talking to his big brother on the phone. Dammit, why should that be? They were brothers, for God's sake. Yeah, Mark had acted like a horse's ass a few times around him, but that was twenty-some years ago. Wasn't it time for them both to get past that? Jim was the older brother, he should take the initiative on that, shouldn't he? Well, what the hell, there was no law that said the younger brother couldn't reach out first. What would his dad have said? Mark knew that almost without thinking of it. He sighed, clicked on the SEND button, and brought up a fresh screen. He'd do it, and when he rotated back home, he'd make a point of visiting Jim, and they'd have a talk.

There was a knock on the flimsy door of Mark's office. "Yeah," he said.

It was Lieutenant Reeves, one of the staff on duty today. "Sir, got a message here from Lieutenant Winkler, Company C." He handed Mark a folded piece of paper.

"Very well, thank you," Mark said. The door closed shut behind Reeves as Mark unfolded the message. *Re that issue you brought up after chapel, the men asked to resolve their differences in the ring. Your presence requested, 1600. Winkler, Co C commanding.*

One of the larger buildings on the base had been converted into a gym, and one of the few thing's Mark's predecessor did right was to keep it in first-rate shape. A fitness nut himself, the guy insisted that all the men have regular PT, to the detriment of their regular training and personal down time. Mark was as much a believer in physical training as anyone else, but he had dialed that back a bit and increased emphasis on doing what they were really here to do. But he appreciated the gym and came over two or three times a week himself.

They had some free weights and a half dozen Total Gym machines Chuck Norris had donated during his last visit downrange. As always, it was a busy place, but most of the crowd now seemed to be gathering around the boxing ring that had been built on the other half of the floor. Two men were in the ring, in opposite corners. One of them was a white guy, solidly built, close-cropped red hair, wearing black twelve-ounce gloves, a tank-top shirt with a biker logo on it, knee-length shorts, and no shoes or socks. The other was shorter, Asian, also barefoot, wearing loose-fitting pants, red MMA-style gloves and no shirt. The kid probably didn't weigh more than a buck-fifty but he was ripped. Mark hadn't seen a physique like that in a while.

Winkler was there, saw Mark and hustled over. "Good afternoon, Colonel."

"What've we got here, Gerard?"

"Well, sir, I discussed the matter with Private Hong, and then with Specialist Rue over there. From what I was able to find out, he's been the one giving Hong a hard time."

"I heard that there were a few guys involved in it."

"Rue would be the instigator, sir. He's been on report once or twice." Mark recalled the name now, seeing it on the weekly reports of disciplinary problems he received from his company commanders. Fortunately, those lists were usually quite short.

"I'd thought Rue was coming around, but things started sliding again when Hong arrived a couple weeks ago."

"Okay, now what?"

"Personal combat, sir. Both men agreed."

Mark sighed. He didn't like this sort of thing, had considered banning it, but it didn't come around very often. As long as it was kept under control and both men shook hands at the end, he'd decided to tolerate it, although he emphasized to his lieutenants that this was not the preferred way to handle disputes among the men. Usually they resolved things themselves with a touch football game, one-on-one basketball, something a little less aggressive, but occasionally it came down to the ring.

"All right. What are the rules?"

"Martial arts sparring, sir, similar to Olympic taekwondo. Two rounds, two minutes each. A punch is worth one point, a kick gets two. Nothing below the belt. No grappling. Sergeant Callahan has some experience with this, so he's the referee."

"I didn't know Rue was a martial arts guy."

Winkler smiled. "He isn't, sir. Says he did some tough-man smokers back home in Wyoming, and I've seen him working out here, sparring with some of the boys."

"What about Hong?"

Winkler's grin got a bit wider. "He wouldn't say, sir, other than that he has some taekwondo background, but another fellow told me Hong's a second-degree black belt."

A bell rang, and a large black soldier in cammie pants and black tee got into the ring, summoned both fighters to the center and started going over the rules. Men had gathered around the ring, two ranks deep now. Mark and Winkler stood toward the back, maybe fifteen feet from the near side of the ring.

Outside each corner stood a soldier holding a white cloth in one hand, a red one in the other.

Callahan moved the two fighters about six feet apart, then signaled to two men at ringside to his left. "Continuous fighting. One point for a punch, two for a kick. Judges, raise the hand with the appropriate color when you see a point. Wave the flag for two points. Scorekeeper, the point is scored when at least three judges concur. Private Hong is red. Timer ready? Scorekeeper ready?" Nods in return, and the sergeant looked quickly at each corner man. "Judges ready?" More nods. "Fighters ready?" Mark noticed both men had mouth guards. Rue had a cheering section, some of the beefier guys on the base, all white, while most of the crowd seemed to be outwardly backing the Korean. Evidently Rue hadn't done a lot to make himself popular.

"*Si jak!*"

It was over in fifteen seconds. Rue stepped in with a right that would've taken Hong's head off if it had been there, but the Korean ducked and weaved with a fluidity Mark had never seen, even in the movies. A leg flashed out and Rue grunted as he staggered backward from the blow to the gut. All four judges shot up the hand with the red flag. Another kick, this one from the other leg as Hong whipped his body around, caught Rue flush in the chest and slammed him back into the ropes. More red flags. Hong timed it perfectly as Rue came back off the ropes on legs that were turning to rubber, and the Korean screamed as one foot rocketed around and upward, catching Rue flush on the right side of his head. Rue's mouthguard spurted out and into the crowd as the big redhead turned a slow, ungainly pirouette and slammed onto the mat.

Callahan rushed over as Hong danced away, perspiration sheening that marvelously cut upper body. The sergeant started counting in Korean as Hong went to the far side of the ring and knelt down, his back to the center. Rue groaned and rolled over as Callahan's count reached five, but he didn't get up. *"Rydel!"* Eight. Callahan waved his arms and a roar came from the crowd. Hong bounced up and walked calmly to the center, where Callahan raised his right arm, shouting *"Sung!"*

Winkler was cheering and applauding alongside Mark. "How about that, Colonel?"

"Pretty impressive," Mark agreed, pleased to see Rue getting slowly to his feet. The beaten man shook his head to clear the cobwebs, then walked toward Hong, stopped, and bowed. Hong returned the bow as the men cheered, and the fighters embraced. Mark joined in the cheering this time.

He noticed Ruiz beside him. "Got here just in time for the bout," the major said. "Colonel, remember that suggestion we got last week about having martial arts classes on the base? I think we might just have found our instructor."

"All right, see if he's interested."

The fighters were leaving the ring now, both surrounded by fellow soldiers congratulating them. Hong looked calm but Mark could see his eyes shining. Rue was starting to come around. He'd have a helluva headache and probably a black eye in the morning, but hopefully this would be an attitude adjustment for him.

"Didn't you tell me your brother does this type of thing?" Ruiz asked.

"Yes," Mark said. "I've heard he's pretty good."

"Oh, and Colonel, I took a call from the General just before I came over here. He wants you to call him back at your earliest convenience."

"Is it urgent?"

"Didn't say so, sir. His aide said when you've got a moment."

Back at the HQ building, Mark told the commo officer on duty to place the call to the General at ISAF in Kabul. "I'll take it in my office."

The phone rang sixty seconds after he took his seat behind his sparse desk. Through the clicks and pops and hisses that marked typical Afghan telephone service, backed up by NATO security features, Mark heard the familiar voice. "Hope I didn't interrupt your Sunday, Mark."

"Not at all, sir."

"Good. This is a somewhat personal call, but it could develop into something requiring your direct participation."

"All right."

Five minutes later, Mark hung up the phone, still stunned. He sat back in his chair, exhaling slowly, replaying the conversation in his mind. He looked down at the notes he'd been scratching on the pad he always kept handy, then realized they'd have to be burned. Bits and pieces of the phone call kept bumping around. He felt another headache coming on.

His brother was in the middle of a CIA operation, flying to Somalia to meet with some terrorist leader, who had gone to college with Jim back in Wisconsin. Unbelievable as that sounded, the guy apparently wanted to defect, and only to Jim. The General expected actionable intel out of the op and it might involve Mark sending some of his people across the border into Pakistan, or a strike team might even be heading into Iran.

"This is close-hold, Mark. I'm letting you know now because of who's involved."

"The meeting will be in Somalia in a few days. I don't have all

the details yet, but DCI gave me a heads-up because if we get any actionable intel, I may have to send a strike team. If the NCA directs, it might be a cross-border operation."

"DCI told me to get my best people ready. I'll need someone I can trust to be on that team, Mark. That's you. I'm getting two teams ready, one for in-country operations, the other will be for the cross-border strike if it comes to that. We have a special unit for that type of thing. You worked with a couple of them from the Legion. I'll brief you in with them in Kabul if we get that far."

"I know he's your brother, Mark, but DCI assures me he'll be in good hands. He'll do all right."

Mark rubbed his temples. What the hell had his big brother gotten himself into?

CHAPTER TWENTY-TWO
WISCONSIN

I T WAS THE phone call that worried him the most, and wasn't that a laugh? He was packing a bag to go to Africa and maybe get killed, and he was worried about calling his boss and asking for emergency leave. There was a policy about getting that, but he couldn't find his company handbook at the moment, so he would just have to wing it.

The phone was in his hand, but he hesitated, looking back at the CIA agent. Allenson was sitting patiently on his couch, while Spears, the G-man, was looking through Jim's bookcase. "We have to leave tonight?" Jim asked.

"I'm afraid so," Allenson said. "We have a plane waiting at O'Hare." She looked at her watch. "We really need to be going pretty soon, Mr. Hayes."

Jim sighed, then looked at his address book, punching in Lori's home number. Maybe he'd get lucky, get her voice mail, just leave a message and be done with it. There would be hell to pay when he got back, but maybe these people could get him a letter from someone in the government, maybe a Cabinet secreta—

"Hello?"

"Uh, Lori, this is Jim Hayes, sorry to bother you at home."

"That's all right, Jim. What can I do for you?" She actually sounded chipper today. Maybe this wouldn't be so bad after all.

"Something has come up, a family emergency. I have to leave town for several days." There was silence. "Are you there?"

"Yes, Jim, I am. You'll be out of town, you said?"

"Yes, I have to catch a plane in a few hours."

Another couple beats of nothing, then, "Might I ask, does this involve your daughter?"

"No, it doesn't," he said, remembering that he had to make one more call tonight. That one would be a lot tougher. "It's about my brother, actually." That was a bit of a white lie, wasn't it? "I really can't say anything more, but I'll be gone at least a week."

There was silence on the other end, then, "I understand there can be emergencies, Jim, but this is a little irregular..."

"Look, if you're concerned about the project, I've got an e-mail ready to send out to Vicki. She can coordinate my files and keep things going, and call Stacy if she needs help." Vicki Johnson was a customer service rep at the co-op who had also worked with Jim on some marketing projects in the past. She hadn't been in the loop on this job, but Jim had no doubt she could get up to speed quickly, and even though Stacy was home with her new baby, she could certainly give good advice by phone, maybe even come in to help out for a day or so. "I already have the draft done. Vicki won't have a problem."

"Not that I don't sympathize with your problem, Jim, but this is a big project, and I just want to make sure it's done right."

4. Prepare the dressing in a small bowl by whisking together the lemon j uice,

5. mayonnaise, onion, Worcestershire sauce, curry and

6. Sea salt and pepper. Pour over salad and toss well.

Fontana Chicken Pesto Pizza

Serves 4

What you need:

1 (12 inch) pre-baked pizza crust

1/2 cup pesto basil sauce

2 cups cooked chicken breast strips

1/2 cup shredded fontina cheese.

1 (6 ounce) jar artichoke hearts, drained

Directions:

1.   Preheat the oven to 450 º F (230 º C).

2.   Spread pesto sauce over the pizza crust.

3.   Arrange chicken pieces and artichoke hearts over the sauce, and sprinkl e with cheese.

4.   Bake for 8 to 10 minute in the preheated oven, until cheese is melted an d lightly browned at the edges.

Black Bean Pizza

What you need:

1 tbsp. vegetable oil

1 (10 ounce) can refrigerated pizza crust

1 1/2 cups shredded Mexican blend cheese, divided.

1 medium onion, chopped

1 garlic clove, minced

1/2 cup finely chopped zucchini

1 (15 ounce) can black beans, rinsed and drained

1 (14.5 ounce) can Italian diced tomatoes, undrained

How you make it:

1. Press dough into a greased 15-in. x 10-in. x 1-in. baking pan. Bake at 425 ° F for 4-6 minutes or until crust just begins to brown.

2. Meanwhile, in a skillet, saute the onion and garlic in oil until tender.

3. Add zucchini; cook and stir for 1 minute. Add the beans and tomatoes; bring to a boil. Boil, uncovered, for 2 minutes; drain.

4. Sprinkle 2/3 cup of cheese over crust.

5. Top with bean mixture and remaining cheese. Bake 8-10 minutes longer or until crust is browned and cheese is melted.

Ultimate Fried Eggs

Serves 2

What you need:

4 Free-range eggs

1 Tablespoon nut almond butter

½ Teaspoon sea salt

1/8 Teaspoon marjoram

1/8 Teaspoon pepper

½ Teaspoon parsley

2 Teaspoons red wine vinegar

How you prepare it:

1. Break the free-range eggs into skillet over half Tablespoon melted almond butter.

2. Add spices and cook until whites are solid.

3. Place eggs onto serving plates.

4. Heat for two minutes, after melting remaining half Tablespoon of almond butter.

5. Stir in red wine vinegar and allow mixture to cook for another minute.

6. Pour over eggs.

7. Garnish with parsley and serve.

Lime Broiled Catfish

Serves 2

What you need:

1/4 teaspoon pepper

1 tablespoon margarine

2 tablespoons lime juice

2 catfish fillets (6 ounces each)

1/4 teaspoon garlic powder

How you prepare it:

1. In a saucepan, melt margarine.
2. Stir in pepper, lime juice and garlic powder; mix well.
3. Remove from heat and set aside.
4. In a shallow baking dish, place fillets.
5. Brush each generously with lime sauce.

6. Broil until fish flakes easily with a fork or for about 5-8 minutes.

7. Remove to a warm serving dish; spoon pan juices over each fillet.

Serves 6

What you need

1 2-3 lbs. pumpkin

2 lbs. medium shrimp

3 cloves garlic

2 large yellow onions, chopped

2 bunches cilantro

4 large plum tomatoes

Tabasco Sauce, to taste

Olive oil for sautéing

Sea salt and pepper

How you prepare it:

1. Line a roasting pan with heavy foil.

2. Preheat oven to 350.

3. Slice off top of pumpkin and save to use as cover/lid.

4. Take out pumpkin strings and seeds.

5. Sauté chopped onions till translucent and beginning to caramelize in the olive oil.

6. Chop and add garlic to the onions.

7. Add freshly ground pepper and sea salt.

8. Clean and devein shrimp.

9. Chop tomatoes and sauté with garlic and onions till the tomatoes have softened.

10. Add shrimp and sauté until shrimp turn pink.

11. Ensure not to overcook!! Chop the cilantro and sprinkle over the shrimp mixture.

12. Taste for sea salt and pepper.

13. Fill the pumpkin with the shrimp mixture. Cover with lid.

14. Bake until the pumpkin is soft. Dish out pumpkin and shrimp together.

Brown's Simple but Delicious Fish

Serves 2

What you need:

1 tsp. dried dill

2 Rainbow trout or salmon fillets

1 tbsp. coarse brown mustard

1/2 cup heavy cream

How you prepare it:

1. Mix mustard, cream, and dill.

2. Pour over fish and bake for 20-30 minutes (depending on thickness of fish), in 375 degree oven until fish is just flaky in center.

3. Do not overcook!

Crunchy Vegetables with Chicken

Serves 4

What you need:

1 teaspoon dark sesame oil

3/4 pound skinned, boned chicken breast, cut into 1-inch pieces

1/4 cup low-sodium teriyaki sauce, divided

1 cup diagonally sliced celery

1 clove garlic, crushed

3/4 cup thinly sliced carrot

1 (8-ounce) can sliced water chestnuts, drained

1 cup coarsely shredded red cabbage

How you prepare it:

1. In a bowl, combine chicken and 1 tablespoon teriyaki sauce; stir well.

2. Let stand 10 minutes.

3. Heat oil in a nonstick skillet over medium-high heat. Add carrot, celery, and garlic; stir-fry 1 minute.

4. Stir in cabbage and water chestnuts; remove from skillet.

5. Add chicken; stir-fry 3 minutes. Add remaining teriyaki sauce; stir-fry 1 minute.

6. Return cabbage mixture to skillet; stir-fry 1 minute or until done.

7. Yield: 4 servings (serving size: 1 cup).

Balsamic Pepper Chicken

Serves 4

What you need:

2 tsp. Extra-virgin olive oil

4 boneless skinless chicken breasts

1/3 cup balsamic vinegar

2 tsp. lemon pepper

2 cloves garlic, minced

1/4 cup chicken stock

How you prepare it:

1. On both sides of the chicken, sprinkle lemon pepper.

2. Heat oil over medium heat, in a skillet.

3. Add chicken and cook until chicken is no longer pink inside, or for about 5-7 minutes on each side.

4. Remove chicken to a serving platter and keep it warm.

5. Mix broth, vinegar, and garlic and add to the skillet.

6. Stir cook over medium-high heat until the mixture is reduced and slightly thickened, or for about 2 minutes. Pour sauce over chicken breasts and serve.

Tip: You can double the sauce ingredients if you want extra sauce for dipping.

Mushroom Chicken

Serves 6

What you need:

12 chicken thighs

Paprika

Sea salt and Pepper

Sauce:

1/2 pound mushrooms, sliced

1/4 cup almond butter

3/4 cup whipping cream

1 tbsp. almond flour

1 tsp. soy sauce

How you prepare it:

1. Preheat oven to 350 F.

2. On a rack over a large cookie sheet, place chicken thighs.

3. Season with sea salt and pepper to taste. Generously dust with paprika.

4. Bake for 1 hr. To make sauce, melt almond butter in large skillet.

5. Add mushrooms; sprinkle with flour, toss mushrooms to distribute flour.

6. Sauté over medium heat, stirring occasionally for 8 to 10 minutes.

7. Add soy sauce, and slowly stir in cream.

8. Cook and stir till mixture bubbles and thickens.

9. Season to taste with sea salt and pepper.

10. Serve over baked chicken thighs.

Chicken Parmesan

Serves 4

What you need:

1 egg, slightly beaten

4 boneless and skinless chicken breast halves

1/2 cup crushed pork rinds

1/2 cup tomato sauce

2 tbsp. Almond butter

1/2 cup Shredded mozzarella cheese

1/4 cup Chopped fresh parsley

1 tbsp. Grated Parmesan cheese

How you prepare it:

1. Flatten chicken to even thickness, using palm of hand.

2. Dip chicken into egg then into crumbs to coat.

3. In skillet over medium heat, in hot margarine, brown chicken on both sides.

4. Add tomato sauce. Reduce heat. Cover; simmer 10 minutes.

5. Sprinkle with cheeses and parsley. Cover; simmer until cheese melts, about 5 minutes.

Almond Chicken Salad

Serves 4-6

What you need:

4 cups cubed cooked chicken

1 cup chopped celery

1 1/2 cups seedless green grapes

3/4 cup sliced green onion

3 free-range eggs, chopped

1/2 cup almond butter

1/2 tsp. pepper

1/4 cup sour cream

1 Tbsp. prepared mustard

1 tsp. sea salt

1/4 tsp. onion pepper

1/4 tsp. celery sea salt

1/8 tsp. dry mustard

1/8 tsp. paprika

1 kiwifruit, peeled and sliced (optional)

1/2 cup slivered almonds, toasted

How you prepare it:

1. Combine grapes, celery, onions, chicken, and eggs, in large bowl.

2. Combine the other nine ingredients, in another bowl; stir unti smooth.

3. Pour over chicken mixture and toss gently.

4. Stir in almonds and serve immediately, or refrigerate and add almonds right before serving.

5. Garnish with kiwifruit if desired.

Smoky Salmon Spread

Serves 4

What you need:

2 8-oz packages cream cheese

2 6-oz cans boneless, skinless pink salmon

3 Tbs. lemon juice

1 tsp. dill weed

3 Tbs. cream

3-4 drops liquid smoke flavoring

Pork skins

1/4 cup green onions

How you prepare it:

1. Drain salmon. Beat cream cheese with lemon juice, cream and dill weed in mixer until light and fluffy.
2. Beat in green onions and salmon until thoroughly combined.
3. Season with liquid smoke to taste.
4. Before serving, chill several hours to allow flavors to blend.
5. Spread on pork skins, to serve.

Macadamia Nut Chicken

Serves 4

What you need:

1 free-range egg

4-6 chicken or fish cutlets

1 cup Macadamia nut crumbs

1/2 cup Macadamia nut oil (or an olive oil/almond butter combination)

2 tbsp. lemon juice

Fresh chopped parsley

Sea salt and pepper

How you prepare it:

1. Dry the roll and cutlets in seasoned flour.

2. Cover cutlets with beaten free-range egg and roll in Macadamia nut crumbs.

3.   Heat oil in pan and fry cutlets gently until light brown either side.

4.   Add lemon juice and continue cooking for 5 minutes.

5.   Serve garnished with parsley.

Sesame Green Beans

Serves 6

What you need:

3/4 pound fresh green beans

1/2 cup water

1 Tablespoon Almond butter

1 Tablespoon soy sauce

2 teaspoons of sesame seeds, toasted

How you prepare it:

1. In a saucepan, bring beans and water to a boil; reduce heat to medium.

2. Cover and cook until the beans are crisp-tender, for about 10-15 minutes; drain.

3. Add soy sauce, almond butter, and sesame seeds; toss to coat.

Serves 4

What you need:

1 cup shredded string beans

8 eggs

I cup sliced mushrooms, canned or fresh

I cup shredded celery

1 1/2 cups shredded cooked chicken

Sea salt and pepper to taste

1 cup shredded onions

How you make it:

1. Place all ingredients in a mixing bowl, combine them thoroughly and divide into 8 portions.

2. Grease well a hot skillet; fry both sides until golden brown.

Delicious Fried Eggs with Red Wine Vinegar

Serves 2

What you need:

4 eggs

1 Tablespoon almond butter

1/8 Teaspoon pepper

½ Teaspoon sea salt

1/8 Teaspoon marjoram

½ Teaspoon parsley

2 Teaspoons red wine vinegar

How you make it:

1.   Break eggs into skillet over ½ Tablespoon melted almond butter.

2.   Add spices and cook until whites are solid.

3.   On your serving plates, place eggs.

4.   Melt remaining ½ Tablespoon of almond butter and heat for 2 min.

5.   Allow mixture to cook for another minute, after stirring in red wine vinegar.

6.   Pour over eggs. Garnish with parsley.

Baked Spiced Chicken

Serves 12

Ginger, onion and garlic are blended in the coating for this easy baked chicken. Yogurt helps keep it moist.

What you need:

1 cup soft bread crumbs

2 fresh whole chickens, cut up

1/2 tsp. onion powder

1/4 tsp. cayenne pepper

1/2 tsp. garlic powder

1/8 tsp. ground ginger

1/3 cup plain yogurt

How you make it:

1. Preheat oven to 350°F.

2. Lightly spray a medium baking dish with vegetable cooking spray; set aside.

3. Rinse chicken pieces and pat dry.

4. Combine bread crumbs, garlic powder, onion powder, cayenne pepper and ginger, in a shallow bowl.

5. Dip chicken pieces in yogurt, then into crumb mixture.

6. Place in prepared dish. Bake, uncovered, until chicken is tender or for about 45 to 50 minutes.

Shrimp Stir-Fry

Servings: 4

What you need:

1 teaspoon sesame oil

1 teaspoon olive oil

1 clove garlic, grated

2 cups sliced mushrooms

1/2 teaspoon grated fresh ginger

1 cup okra

1/2 cup chopped green peppers

2 cups string beans

1/4 teaspoon ground black pepper

2 cups cleaned cooked shrimp

How you make it:

1. Stir-fry peppers, mushrooms, garlic, and ginger in olive oil and sesame oil until crisp-tender.

2. Meanwhile steam okra and string beans until crisp-tender.

3.   Drain, and add to mushrooms and peppers. Stir in shrimp and pepper until just warmed.

4.   Serve over a bed of lettuce. Enjoy!

Southern Mushroom Soup

Servings: 4

What you need:

1/2 cups chopped fresh mushrooms

1 small onion, chopped

1/2 cups chicken broth

1/2 tablespoons almond butter, melted

1 tablespoons all-purpose flour

1/2 cups milk

1/8 cup heavy cream

1 pinch sea salt and pepper to taste

2 slices white bread, toasted

1/4 tablespoon softened almond butter

1/4 cup shredded sharp Cheddar cheese.

How you make it:

1. In a saucepan, combine the mushrooms, onion and chicken broth.

2. Bring to a boil, then simmer covered for 15 minutes over low heat.

3. Stir together the melted almond butter and flour to make a paste.

4. Stir the paste into the pan with the vegetables.

5. Increase the heat to medium, and gradually stir in the milk.

6. Continue stirring constantly.

7. When the mixture thickens and begins to boil, stir in the cream.

8. Cook over low heat without boiling for about 10 minutes, or until the mushrooms are tender.

9. Season with sea salt and pepper.

10. Ladle the soup into bowls, and trim pieces of toast to fit the bowls.

11. Almond butter the toast, and place on top of the soup.

12. Sprinkle the cheese over the bread and serve.

Thai Chicken Salad

This salad is great with either tuna or chicken. If your taste buds cannot handle chili, use less or leave it out altogether.

Servings: 2

What you need:

2 lettuce leaves (use different kinds)

1/2 tbsp. coriander, chopped

1/2 tbsp. fresh mint, chopped

1/4 orange, peeled and sectioned

1/4 can tuna or 1 chicken breast, cooked and shredded

100 g red seedless grapes, halved

1/8 cucumber, sliced

1/2 small red onion, thinly sliced

Dressing

Zest of 1 lime

Juice of 1 limes

1 garlic cloves

1/2 serrano chilies, halved, seeded and cut into pieces

1/2 tbsp. fish or soy sauce

2 tbsp. cashews, chopped

1/2 tbsp. honey or agave nectar

How you make it:

1. Place half the lettuce in a bowl or on a platter. Tear the rest of the lettuce leaves into bite sizes and add to the bowl or platter.
2. Sprinkle the coriander and mint over the lettuce leaves.
3. Add the orange, tuna or chicken, grapes, cucumber and red onion.
4. Refrigerate this while you make the dressing.
5. Grate the lime zest into a blender or food processor.
6. Add the garlic, chilies, lime juice, fish or soy sauce and honey or agave, and blend until smooth.
7. Pour the dressing over the salad. Garnish with cashews and serve.

Fish with Mediterranean Salsa

Servings: 2

What you need:

1 tsp. extra virgin olive oil

1/2 tsp. dried oregano

2 fish fillets

1 tbsp. water

1/4 tsp. chili powder

1/2 tsp. dried thyme

1/2 tsp. freshly grated lemon zest

1/2 tomato, deseeded and chopped

1/2 (60g) can Kalamata olives or ripe olives, drained and sliced

5 g fresh parsley, chopped

Juice of ½ lemon

1/2 tbsp. capers, drained (optional)

How you make it:

1. Preheat the oven to 160°C or Gas Mark 3.

2. Coat a baking dish with cooking oil spray and arrange the fish in a single layer.

3. Pour the water over the fish and sprinkle with chili powder, thyme and lemon zest. Cover the dish with foil and bake for 15 minutes.

4. Mix the tomato, olives, lemon juice, parsley, capers, oil and oregano thoroughly, in a small bowl.

5. Place the fish on a serving platter, top with the salsa and serve.

Slow Cooker Chicken Curry with Quinoa

Servings: 1-2

What you need:

1/3 cup quinoa

1 1/2 pounds diced chicken breast meat

1 1/4 cups chopped celery

1 3/4 cups chopped Granny Smith apples

3/4 cup chopped onion

1 cup chicken broth

1/4 cup nonfat milk

1 tablespoon curry powder

1/4 teaspoon paprika

How you make it:

1. Place the chicken, onion, celery, apple, chicken broth, milk, curry powder, and paprika into a slow cooker; stir until mixed.

2. Cover, and cook on Low for 4 to 5 hours.

3. Stir in the quinoa during the final 35 minutes of cooking.

4. Serve when quinoa is tender

Quinoa Pudding with Vanilla

Servings: 2

What you need:

1/2 cup quinoa, rinsed

1/8 cup natural cane sugar

1/8 teaspoon ground cardamom

1 cups almond or hemp milk

1/4 cup water

1 teaspoons vanilla extract

Fine sea salt to taste

How you make it:

1. In a medium saucepan, add the quinoa, sugar, cardamom, sea salt, milk, and water over medium heat.
2. Allow the ingredients to reach a boil and then reduce the heat to medium-low.

3. Cover the saucepan with the lid slightly ajar.

4. Simmer the pudding for approximately 30 minutes, stirring occasionally.

5. The quinoa should become very soft and the mixture should have a thick consistency.

6. Remove the quinoa from the heat and stir in the vanilla.

7. Put the pudding in a heatproof bowl and allow it to cool until it reaches room temperature.

Quinoa with Almond Porridge

Servings: 2

What you need:

1 ¼ cups soy or almond milk, divided

½ cup quinoa, rinsed

1 cup water

½ teaspoon ground cinnamon

Drizzle of honey

Dried or fresh fruit, for serving

Pinch of sea sea salt

How you make it:

1. Over medium heat, place a medium saucepan.

2. Add the quinoa and cook.

3. Stir the quinoa for a few minutes until it is toasted.

4. Add 1 cup of the milk, cinnamon, the water, and sea sea salt.

5. Stir the mixture and turn up the heat until it begins to boil.

6. Reduce the heat to low, once the quinoa is boiling.

7. Cook for approximately 25 minutes, while the saucepan is covered.

8. Stir the porridge occasionally until it becomes thick and the quinoa is tender.

9. Drizzle the remaining milk and honey over the porridge and add the fruit before serving.

Thank You

If you follow religiously to The <u>10-Day Green Smoothie Cleanse by JJ Smith</u>. And some of the clean high protein meal provided for you in this book. You are going to be seeing great results in your body and health, because you would lose weight and keep it off for good.

<u>If you enjoyed the recipes in this book, please take the time to share your thoughts and post a positive review with 5 star rating on Amazon, it would encourage me and make me serve you better. It'd be greatly appreciated!</u>

Other Health Related Book You'll Like

Get The 10 Day green Smoothie Cleanse Recipes

10-Day Green Smoothie Cleanse: 41 Yummy Green Smoothies to Help you

Lose Up to 15 Pounds in 10 Days!

Click Here to Buy Now >> http://www.amazon.com/10-Day-Green-Smoothie-

Cleanse-Smoothies-ebook/dp/B00KCYJ4CO

The Tapping Solution for Weight Loss and Body Confidence is a powerful system that releases the emotions and beliefs that hold us back from loving our bodies. I use tapping on a regular basis and have personally benefitted from this powerful method. It's one of the most important practices in my healing arsenal.

Get The **The Ultimate Tapping Solution Guide: Using EFT to Tap your way to WEIGHT LOSS, Wealth and Build Body Confidence for Women**

Click Here>> Amazon U.S Link>> http://www.amazon.com/Ultimate-Tapping-Solution-Guide-Confidence-ebook/dp/B00K6JB97S

Books on Health & Fitness Diets

RECOMMENDED BOOK FOR WEIGHT LOSS AND DIET:

My 10-Day Smoothie Cleanse & Detox Diet Cookbook: Burn the Fat, Lose weight Fast and Boost your Metabolism for Busy Mom, Restart your life with this cookbook and experience an amazing transformation of your body and your health. I am really excited for you!

CLICK HERE TO BUY: **http://www.amazon.com/10-Day-Detox-Diet-Cookbook-Metabolism-ebook/dp/B00IRE3CV0**

Get this bestselling Grain Brain Book- **My brain against all grain Cookbook: 61 Easy-to-make Healthy Foods that would help you stick to the Grain-Brain-free Diet!**

Discover The Surprising Truth about Wheat, Carbs, and Sugar--Your Brain's Silent Killers

Amazon US Link: http://www.amazon.com/dp/B00J9DX3X0

Amazon UK Link: http://www.amazon.co.uk/dp/B00J9DX3X0

The Coconut Diet Cookbook: Using Coconut Oil to Lose weight

FAST, Supercharge Your Metabolism & Look Beautiful!

Link http://www.amazon.com/dp/B00K1II0GS

14532935R00058

Made in the USA
San Bernardino, CA
30 August 2014